T0383469

Published and distributed by
viction:workshop ltd.

viction:ary™

viction:workshop ltd.
Unit C, 7/F, Seabright Plaza, 9–23 Shell Street,
North Point, Hong Kong SAR
Website: www.victionary.com
Email: we@victionary.com
 @victionworkshop
 @victionworkshop
Bē @victionary
 @victionary

Edited and produced by viction:ary

Concepts & art direction by Victor Cheung
Book design by viction:workshop ltd.
Cover image: Fancy Couple by Heiko Müller (also on P. 103)

Fourth Edition
©2022, 2023, 2024, 2025 viction:workshop ltd.
Copyright on published work is held by
respective designers and contributors.

ISBN 978-988-74629-3-4
Printed and bound in China

DARK
INSPIRATION

20TH ANNIVERSARY EDITION

INTRODUCTION

ave you ever shielded your eyes from a terrifying scene during a horror movie, but still felt compelled to look through the cracks of your fingers, curious to see what sort of gruesome image awaits? As morbid, grotesque, and macabre as they may be, the genre of dark illustrations evoke the same unexplainable reaction, with their depictions of haunting portraits, gory situations, and unsettling compositions that leave us inescapably drawn to the horrors that lie within.

From the Eldritchian monstrosities in H. P. Lovecraft's stories to the bone-chilling depictions of the sinister and supernatural occurrences in Junji Ito's manga collection, the human race's fascination with the hideous and horrible has long permeated the sphere of popular culture and contemporary art. Besides the exaggeration of features and disturbing details, the use of macabre thematic imagery and cinematic scene settings are also what strike viewers psychologically at first sight.

Without a clear indication of what "dark" exactly is, its ambiguity leaves viewers to their own interpretations guided by their own feelings and experiences. That is to say that rather than what is directly depicted in these artworks, it is the tone set, combined with the viewer's own imagination and emotions that truly bring the haunting aspect to life. Moreover, the use of thematic imagery, hidden metaphors, and even dark humour is also an abstraction of the artist's beliefs, dreams, and consciousness, opening a portal to understanding each artist's psyche as well as their ways of processing negative and unwholesome parts of life.

Just like the duality of yin and yang, or the other side of the moon, we as humans are always harbouring a delicate balance of light and darkness within. Our attraction to the macabre is perhaps due to the fact that it brings out what we usually tend to suppress. As we lay our eyes on these creations, we are confronted with our own innate desire to indulge in the darkness and are tempted to peer into how grim human nature can truly be.

Similar and often linked to sub-cultures and aesthetics such as goth, emo, or scene, dark art is often regarded as alternative and even deviant for its exploration beyond what is usually depicted in mainstream media — all are a brazen challenge to what is considered "normal" and "standard" in traditional genres of art.

In Amandine Urruty's (P. 084–089) excruciatingly-detailed pencil drawings, the seemingly innocent portraits of children at play reveal a more sinister story upon closer inspection. Featuring subjects donning a facial covering and accompanied by a party of weird, lifelike toys, one would find these pieces surprisingly similar to Victorian-era post-mortem photography, which was a popular way to commemorate the dead, namely stillborn babies or children who suffered a premature death. Despite the grim connotations implied, the unabashed absurdness of the surrounding animals and objects still add a pinch of twisted humour to the works of art as part of Urruty's signature style.

One might find themselves frozen in place as they turn the page to face the piercing stares of Alessandro Bianchi Sicioldr's (P. 070–079) haunting, Renaissance-style oil portraits. Drawing influence from mythology and medieval art, Sicioldr's work also stems from the artist's own nightmares and visions. While the true meaning behind the otherworldly imagery of his paintings remains in the dark, it is certain that his creations will continue to provoke viewers with their individual interpretations.

Viewers may also find themselves transfixed by the mind-bending collage art of Lola Dupre (P. 130–135), who produces her creations by cutting up duplicates of the same image and skilfully pasting them in an intricate pattern that forms visual illusions. The results are often strikingly similar to a real photograph at first glance and not unlike hyperrealistic portraits or paintings. However, laced with a trail of elongated visages, contorted bodies, plus extra limbs, eyes, and mouths, Dupre's creations strike an unnerving chord with their deformed abnormalities and uncanny resemblance to reality.

On the same note, Mia Mäkilä's (P. 058–061) monstrous subjects donning children's frocks make a sharp contrast with their gruesome appearance. Often painted with grisly features such as bloodshot, bulging eyes, rotting flesh, and smiles that resemble a toothy snarl, Makila purposely places these menacing creatures in somehow hilarious scenarios to invoke fear and disgust but also amusement in viewers.

For Nadja Jovanovic (P. 120–129), feelings of unnerving fear and unsettlement are created through a haunting absence, as shown in the depiction of empty eye sockets, toothless mouths, or hollow faces. Bald, handless men clad in black suits, smoke, and water are also common themes in Jovanovic's surreal artworks. Often shown in positions of sinking, suffocation, and drowning, her characters invite viewers to submerge themselves in feelings of despair and a world of nothingness.

Slipping back into reality, Fiona Roberts' (P. 392–399) eerie installations of body parts fused into seemingly ordinary household objects and furniture allow for a tactile sensory experience that disturbs and intrigues at the same time: Multiple mouths open agape on skin stretched over a vintage chair, while a cluster of eyeballs glare maliciously from a crimson plush armchair. A pale winter coat hangs on a peg on the wall, hiding an esophagus with lungs that wraps itself innocuously around the coathanger like a scarf. Aside from its grotesque nature, Roberts' work also carries an air of elegance and beauty hidden within.

As often as we turn to familiar objects and things of beauty, there is also a hidden desire within us to comprehend things that are unfamiliar and repulsive. Darkness does not reside in the art or the artist, but by nature, the subjects that these creations depict. With a collection of disturbing and evocative expressions from our previous two editions, the third instalment of Dark Inspiration collates carefully-selected works by 71 creatives from all corners of the world.

Aside from something to be admired, these evocative artworks are also a mirror that reflects the darkest depths of our consciousness. So, we invite you to turn the page and allow each piece to bring your fears and darkest fantasies out of hiding...who knows what sort of horrors lurk within your own mind?

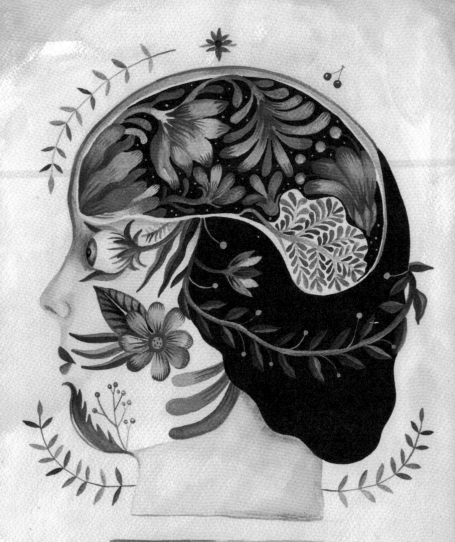

HEAD

F O O T

H A N D

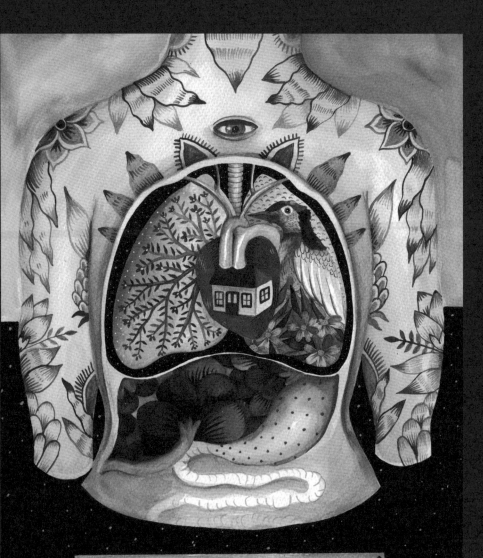

CHEST & ABDOMEN

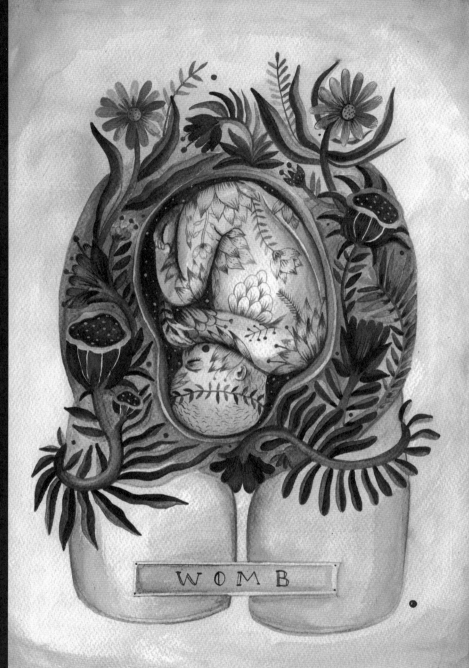

W O M B

HUMAN

BLOOD

SKULL

SKELETON

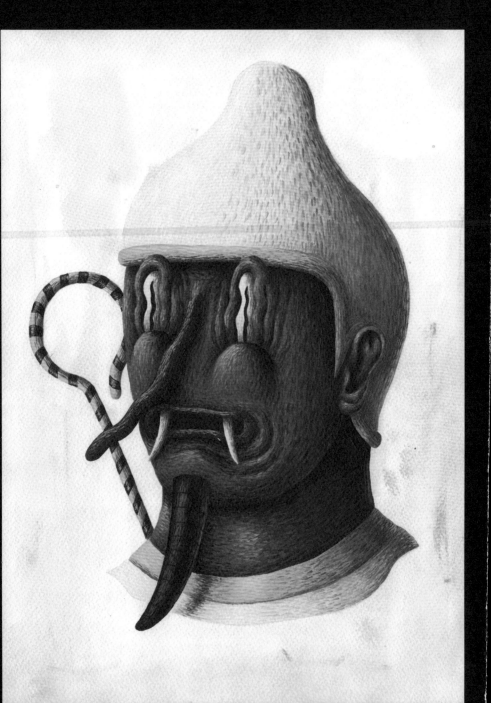

RAUL OPREA AKA SADDO

RAUL OPREA AKA SADDO

PASSAGE OF

JEFF MCMILLAN

JEFF MCMILLAN

MIRANDA MEEKS

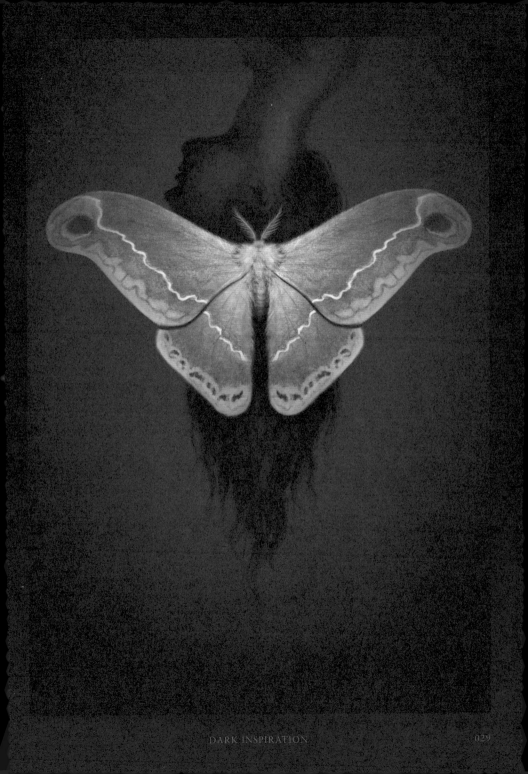

MIRANDA MEEKS

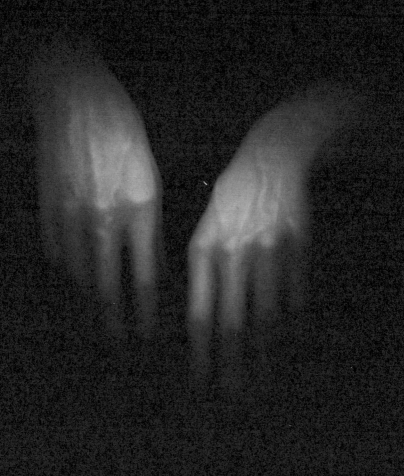

JAMES JEAN

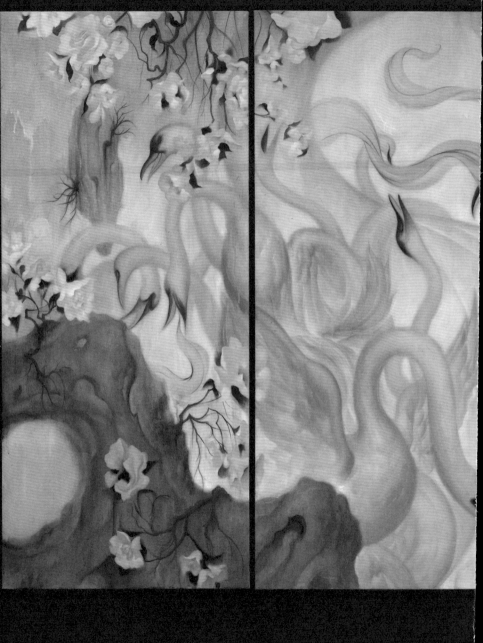

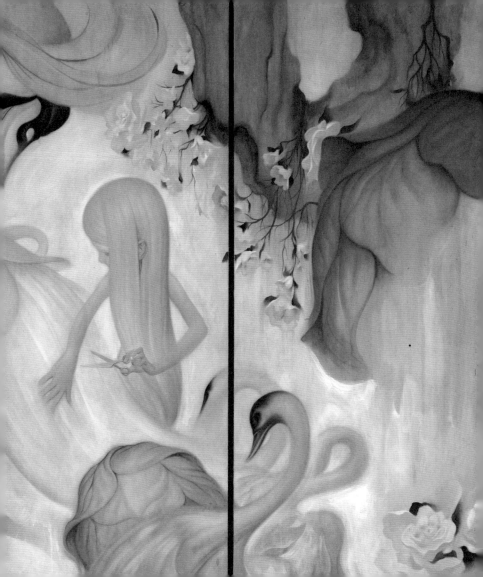

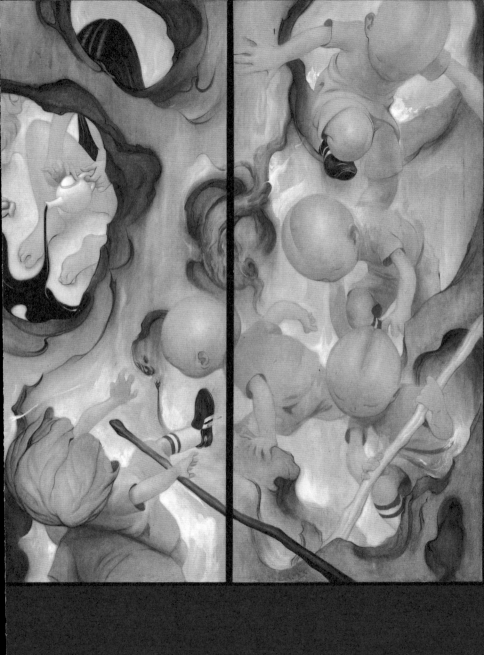

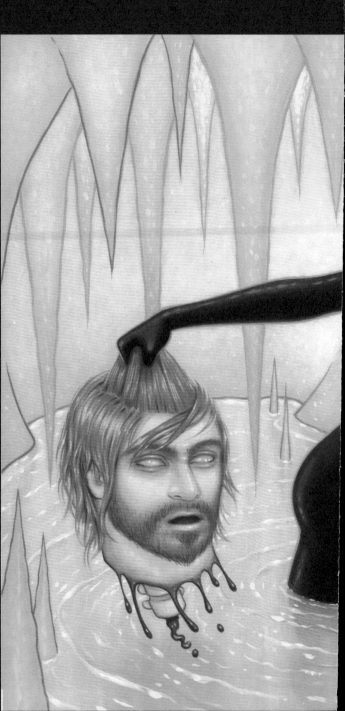

TARA MCPHERSON

BENE ROHLMANN

Kurz darauf...

The youthful shepherdess of this nothing knew,
But went to meet her true love as she used to do:
She search'd the garden all around, but no true love she sound.
At length Bloody Gardener did appear.

What business have you here, madam, I pray?
Are you come here to rob the garden gay ?
Cries she, No theif I am, but wait for that young-man,
Who did this night appoint to meet me here.

He spoke no more, but strait a knife he took,
And pierc'd her heart before one word she spoke,
Then on the ground she tell, crying, Sweet love, farewel.
O welcome, welcome, Death, thy fatal stroke.

Was this done now, my dear; by your design ?
Or by your cruel parents most unkind,
My life is thus betray'd farewell vain world, she said,
I hope in heaven I a place shall find

But when he see her life was really gone,
Immediately he lay'd her in the ground,
With flowers fine and gay her corpse did overlay,
Intending that her body should not be found.

Excerpt from 'The Bloody Gardener's Cruelty;
Or, The Shepherd's Daughter Betray'd.'

There were two sisters, they went playing,
Refrain: With a hie downe downe a downe-a
To see their father's ships come sayling in.
Refrain: With a hy downe downe a downe-a
And when they came unto the sea-brym,
The elder did push the younger in.

'O sister, O sister, take me by the gowne,
And drawe me up upon the dry ground.'
'O sister, O sister, that may not bee,
Till salt and oatmeale grow both of a tree.'

Somtymes she sanke, somtymes she swam,
Until she came unto the mill-dam.
The miller runne hastily downe the cliffe,
And up he betook her withouten her life.'

What did he doe with her brest-bone?
He made him a violl to play thereupon.
What did he doe with her fingers so small?
He made him peggs to his violl withall.

'The Twa Sisters'

KATY HORAN

MIA MÄKILÄ

MIA MÄKILÄ

DAVID HO

DAVID HO

LOSTFISH

ALESSANDRO SICIOLDR BIANCHI

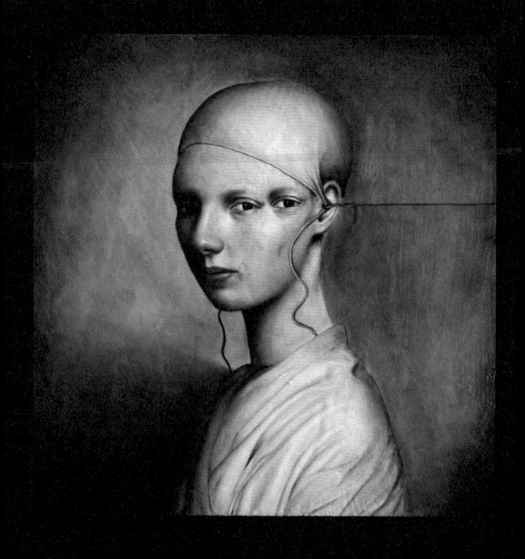

ALESSANDRO SICIOLDR BIANCHI

ALESSANDRO SICIOLDR BIANCHI

 ALESSANDRO SICIOLDR BIANCHI

ALESSANDRO SICIOLDR BIANCHI

AMANDINE URRUTY

DARK INSPIRATION   083

AMANDINE URRUTY

DANNY VAN RYSWYK

DANNY VAN RYSWYK

DANNY VAN RYSWYK

Round about the cauldron go;
In the poison'd entrails throw.
Toad, that under cold stone
Days and nights has thirty-one
Swelter'd venom sleeping got,
Boil thou first i' the charmed pot.

Double, double toil and trouble;
Fire burn, and cauldron bubble.

Fillet of a fenny snake,
In the cauldron boil and bake;
Eye of newt and toe of frog,
Wool of bat and tongue of dog,
Adder's fork and blind-worm's sting,
Lizard's leg and owlet's wing,
For a charm of powerful trouble,
Like a hell-broth boil and bubble.

Double, double toil and trouble;
Fire burn, and cauldron bubble.

Excerpt from Macbeth, Act IV, Scene I
by William Shakespeare

HEIKO MÜLLER

NICOLETTA CECCOLI

NICOLETTA CECC

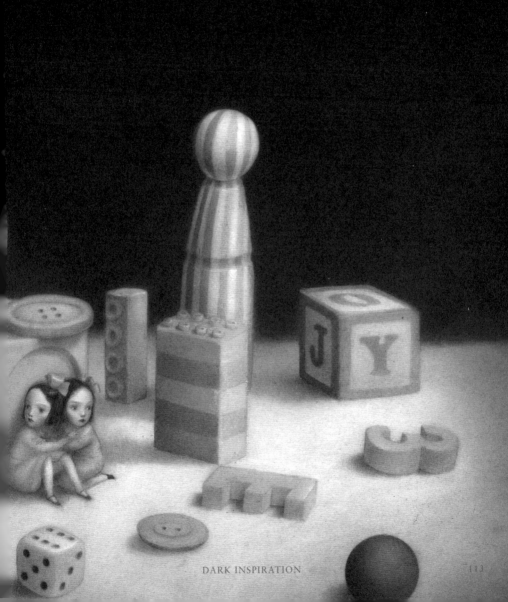

DARK INSPIRATION [115]

NICOLETTA CECCOLI

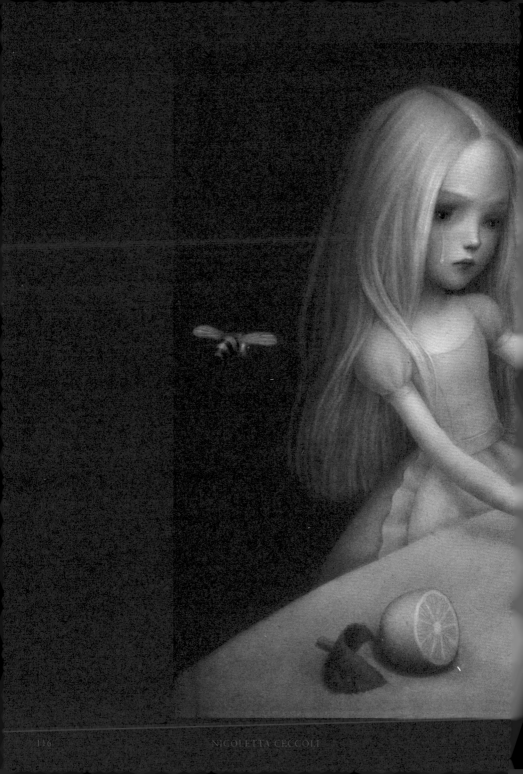

NICOLETTA CECCOLI

NICOLETTA CECCOLI

NADJA JOVANOVIĆ

NADJA JOVANOVIC

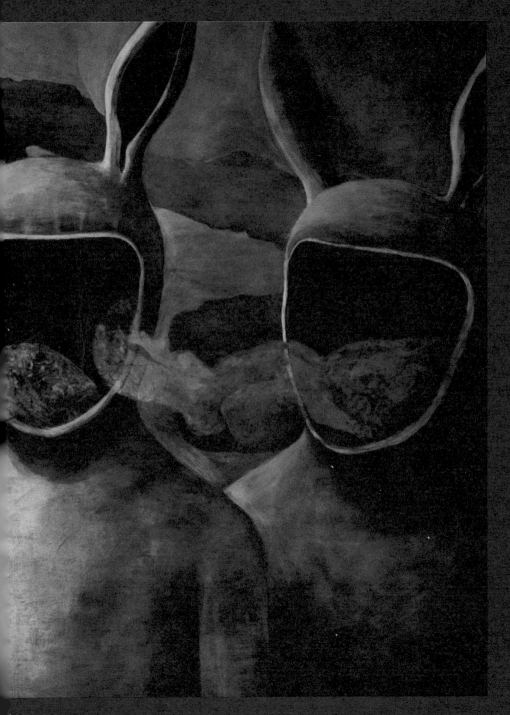

LOLA DUPRE

LOLA DUPRE

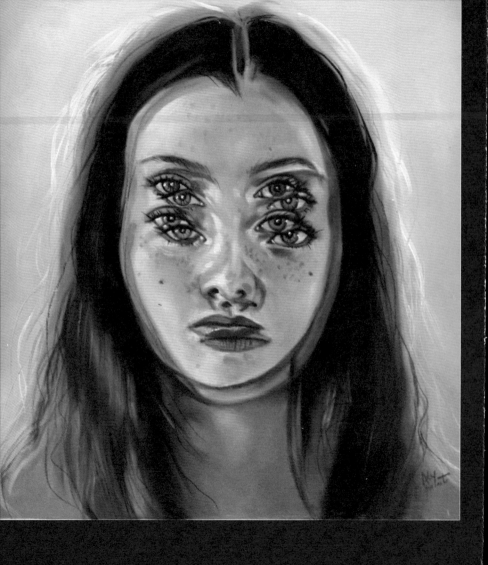

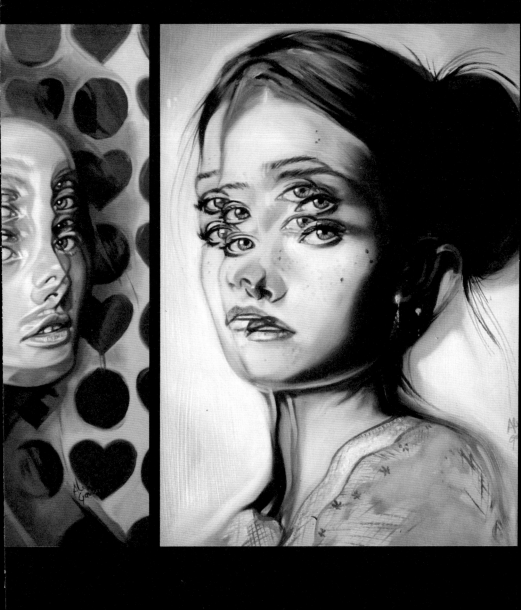

ALEX GARANT

UNI
QLO

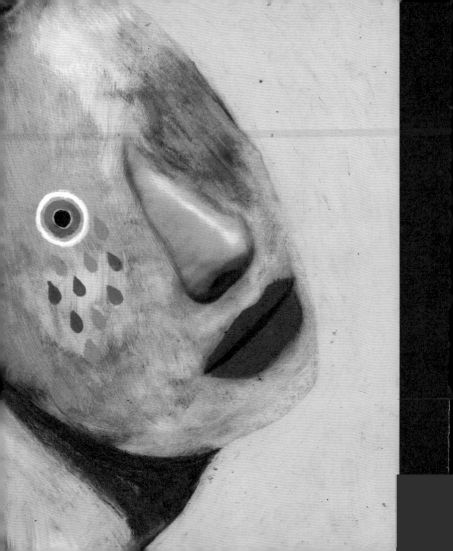

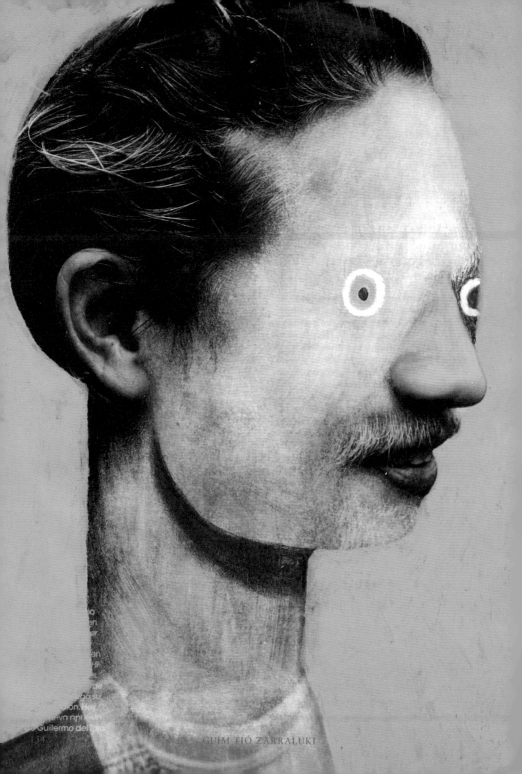

GUIM TIÓ ZARRALUKI

GUIM TIÓ ZARRALUKI

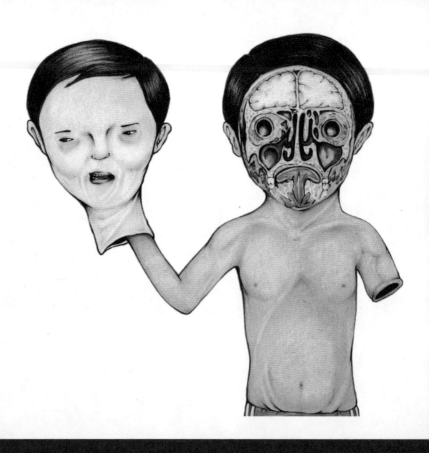

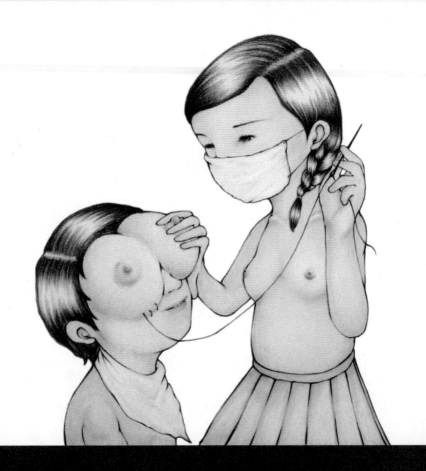

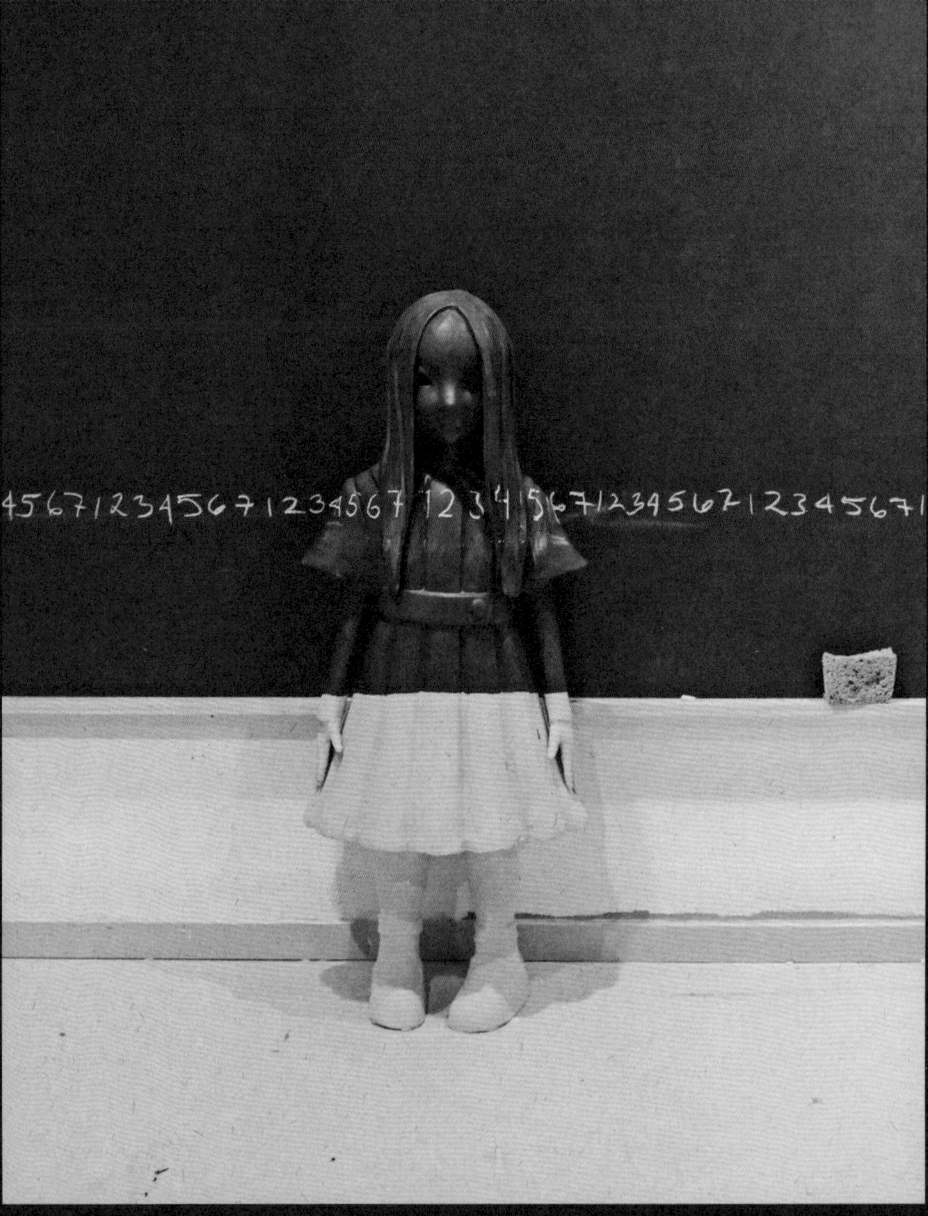

KIM SIMONSSON

KIM SIMONSSON

Prepare, prepare, new guests draw near,
And on the brink of hell appear.

Kindle fresh flames of sulphur there.
Assemble all ye fiends,
Wait for the dreadful ends
Of impious men, who far excel
All th' inhabitants of hell.

Let 'em come, let 'em come,
To an eternal dreadful doom,
Let 'em come, let 'em come.

In mischiefs they have all the damned outdone;
Here they shall weep, and shall unpitied groan,
Here they shall howl, and make eternal moan.

By blood and lust they have deserved so well,
That they shall feel the hottest flames of hell.

In vain they shall here their past mischiefs bew

Eternal darkness they shall find,
And them eternal chains shall bind
To infinite pain of sense and mind.

Let 'em come, let 'em come,
To an eternal dreadful doom,
Let 'em come, let 'em come.

'Song of Devils' by Thomas Shadwell

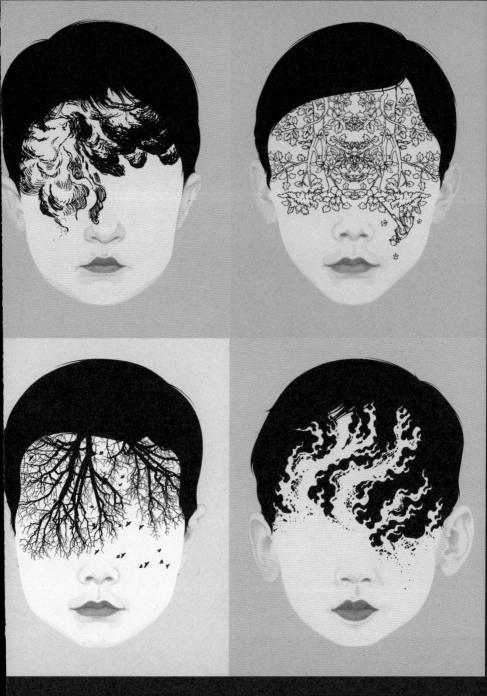

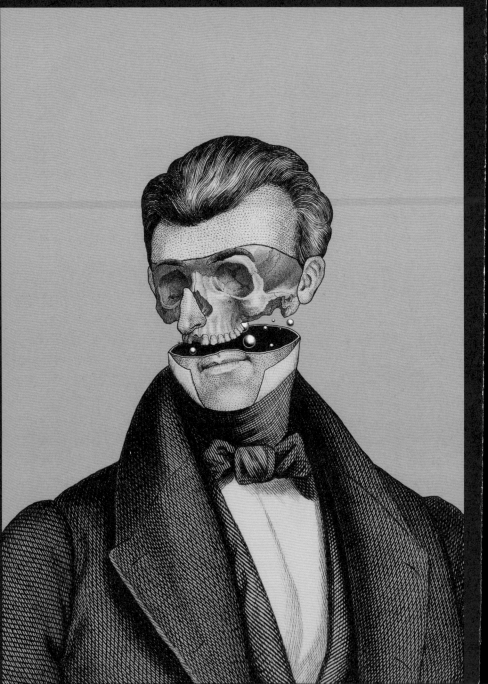

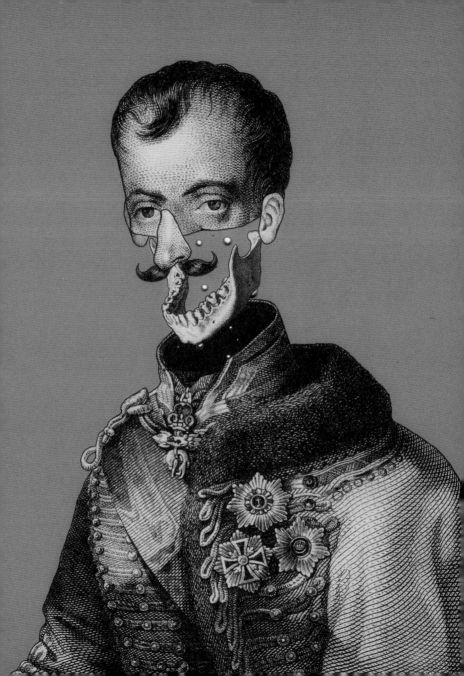

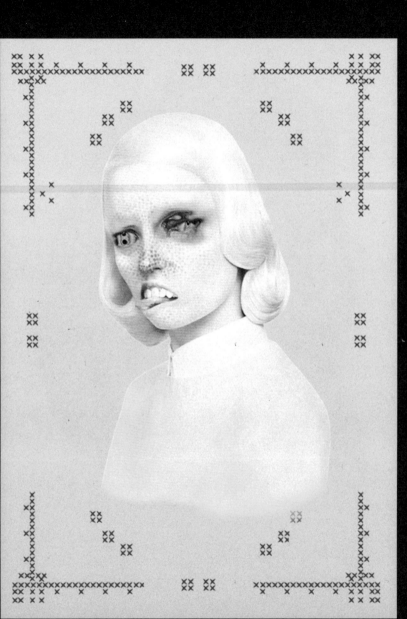

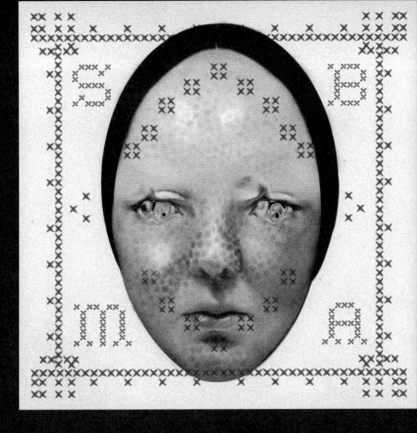

OLEG DOU

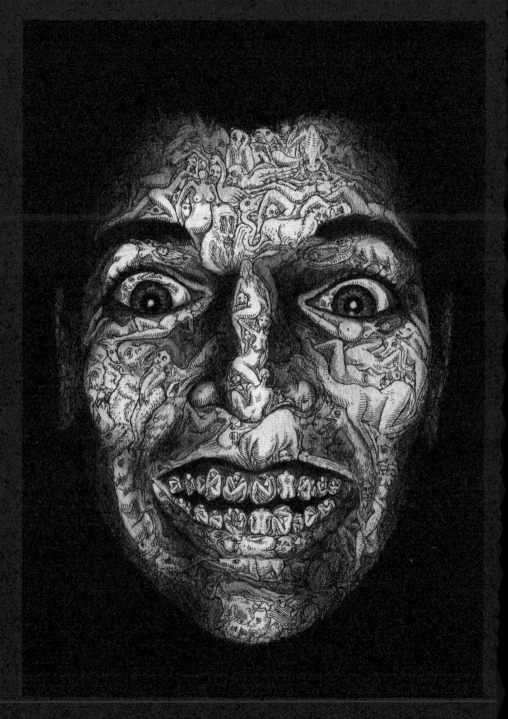

JON BEINART

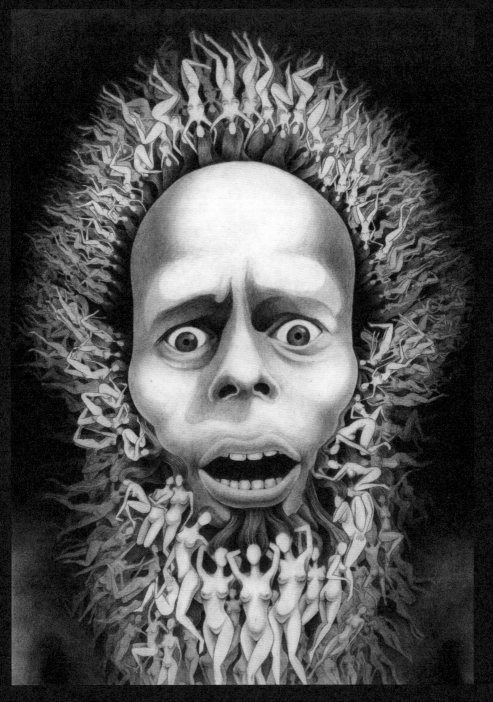

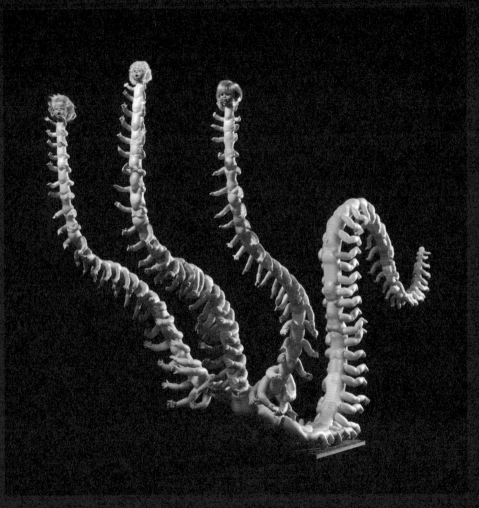

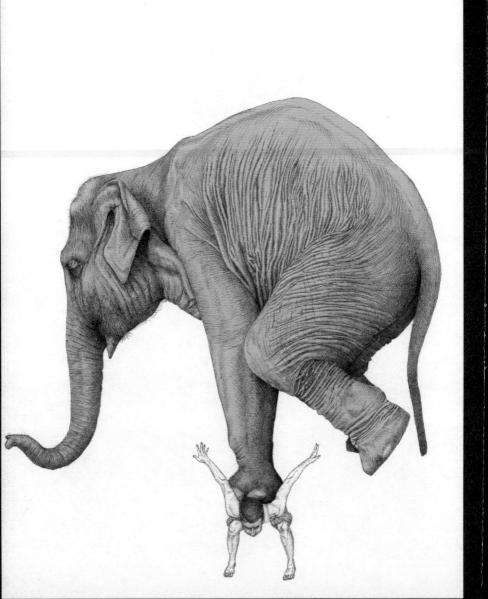

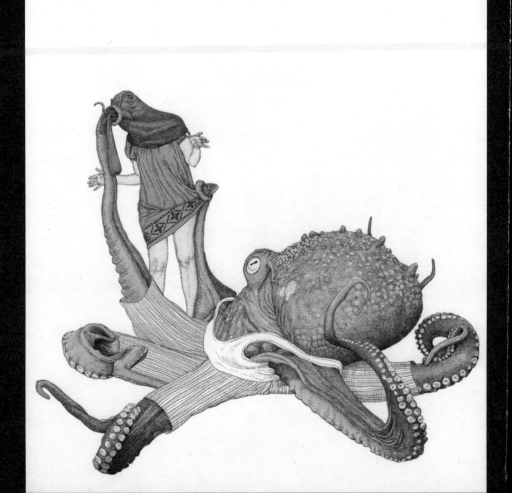

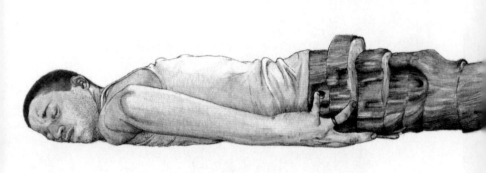

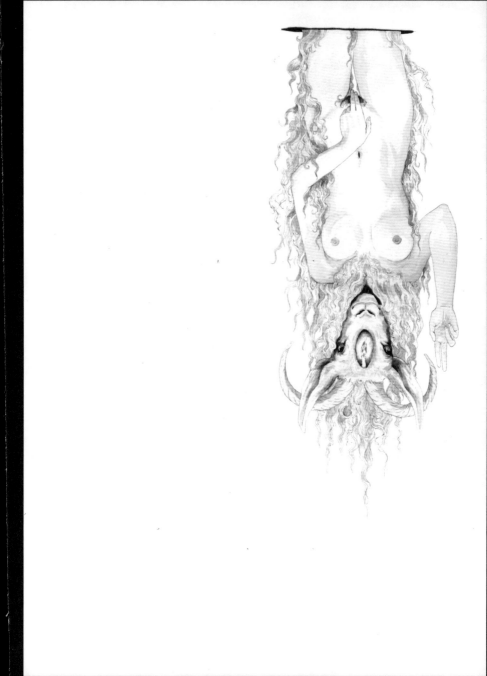

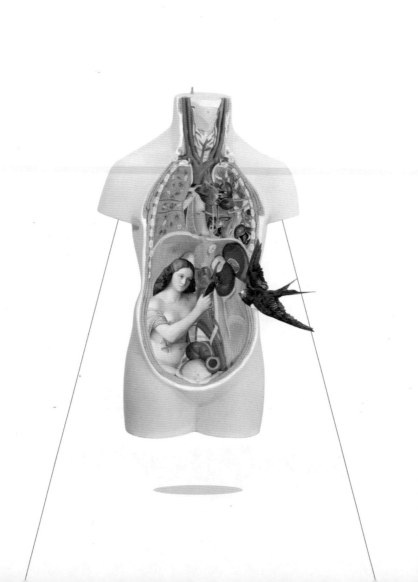

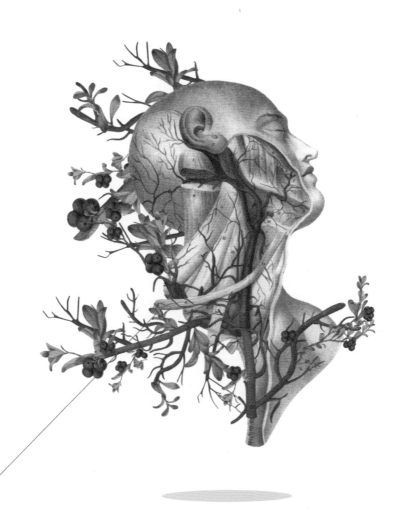

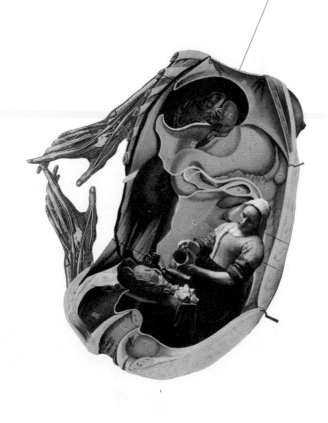

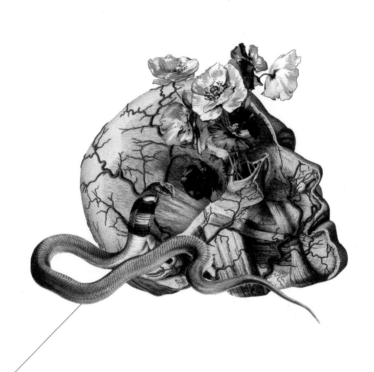

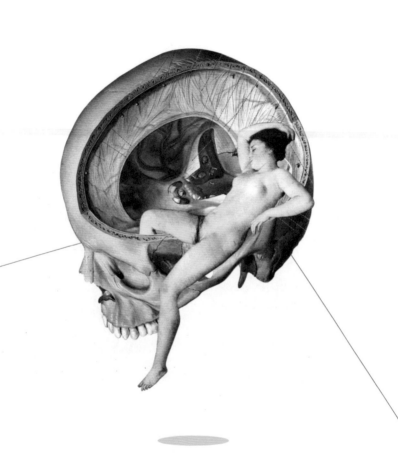

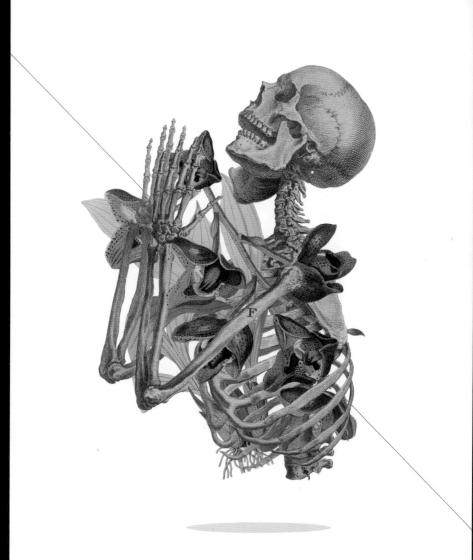

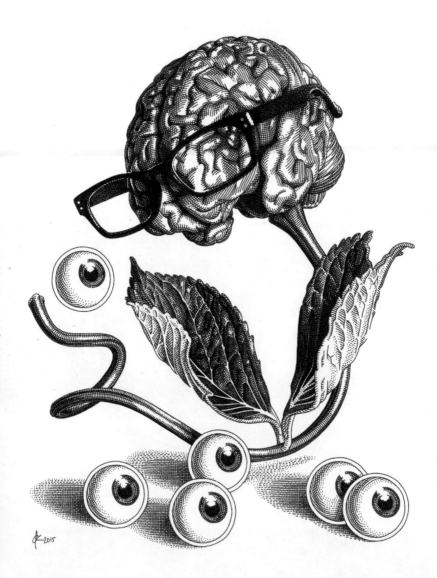

DAN HILLIER

DAN HILLIER

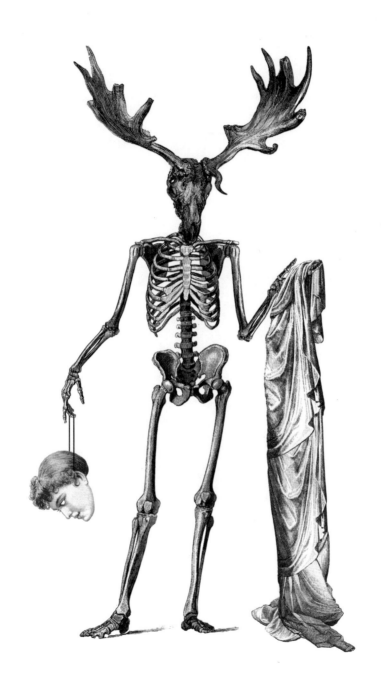

DAN HILLIER

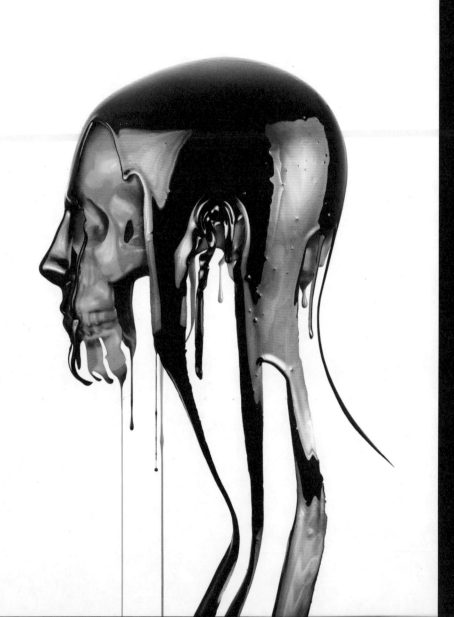

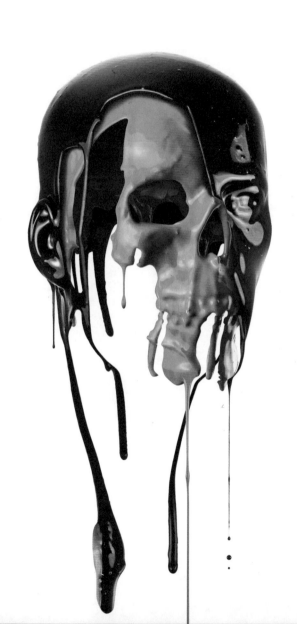

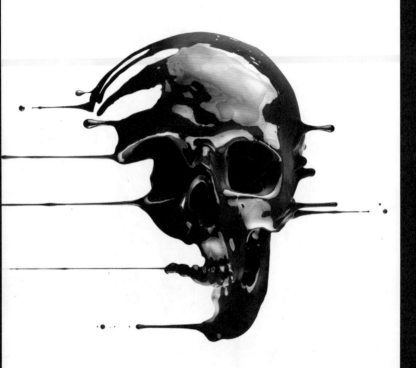

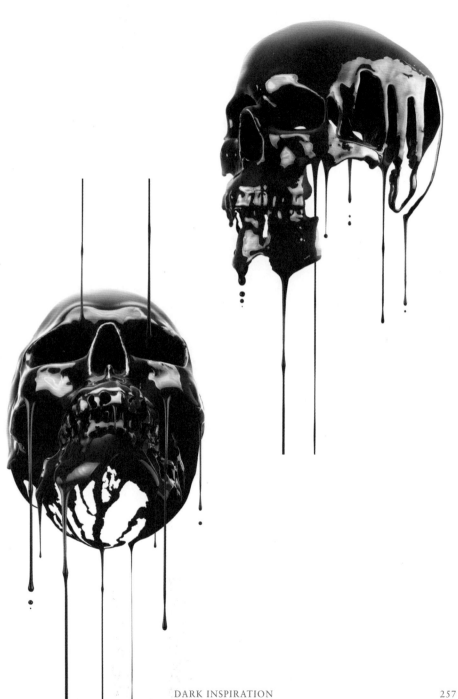

IGNIS   TERRA

DANIEL MARTIN DIAZ

All attitudes, all the shapeliness, all the belongings of my or
    your body or of any one's body, male or female,
The lung-sponges, the stomach-sac, the bowels sweet and clean,
The brain in its folds inside the skull-frame,
Sympathies, heart-valves, palate-valves, sexuality, maternity,
Womanhood, and all that is a woman, and the man that comes
    from woman,
The womb, the teats, nipples, breast-milk, tears, laughter,
    weeping, love-looks, love-perturbations and risings,
The voice, articulation, language, whispering, shouting aloud,
Food, drink, pulse, digestion, sweat, sleep, walking, swimming,
Poise on the hips, leaping, reclining, embracing, arm-curving
    and tightening,
The continual changes of the flex of the mouth, and around
    the eyes,
The skin, the sunburnt shade, freckles, hair,
The curious sympathy one feels when feeling with the hand the
    naked meat of the body,
The circling rivers the breath, and breathing it in and out,
The beauty of the waist, and thence of the hips, and thence
    downward toward the knees,
The thin red jellies within you or within me, the bones and the
    marrow in the bones,
The exquisite realization of health;
O I say these are not the parts and poems of the body only, but
    of the soul,
O I say now these are the soul!

Excerpt from 'I Sing the Body Electric'
by Walt Whitman

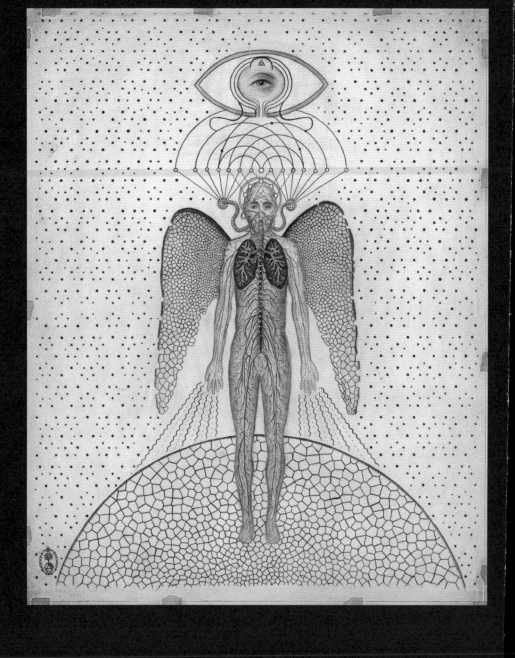

01100111 01101111

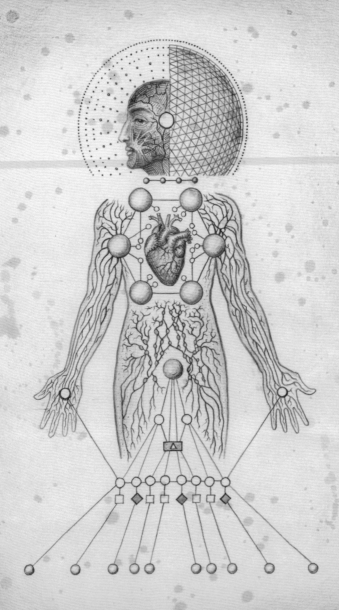

DANIEL MARTIN DIAZ

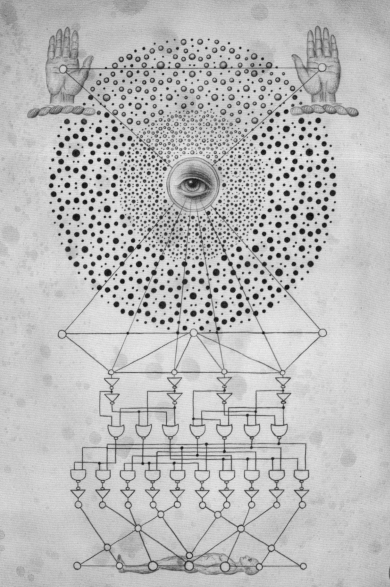

DARK INSPIRATION

DAS SCHÖNSTE, WAS WIR ERLEBEN KÖNNEN, IST DAS GEHEIMNISVOLLE

DANIEL MARTIN DIAZ

AUDREY KAWASAKI

SERGIO MORA / AGENCY RUSH

YURY USTSINAU

YURY USTSINAU

YURY USTSINAU

TIM LEE

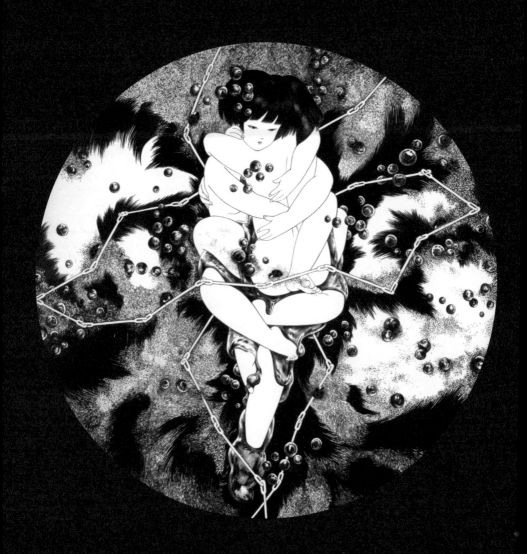

AKINO KONDOH

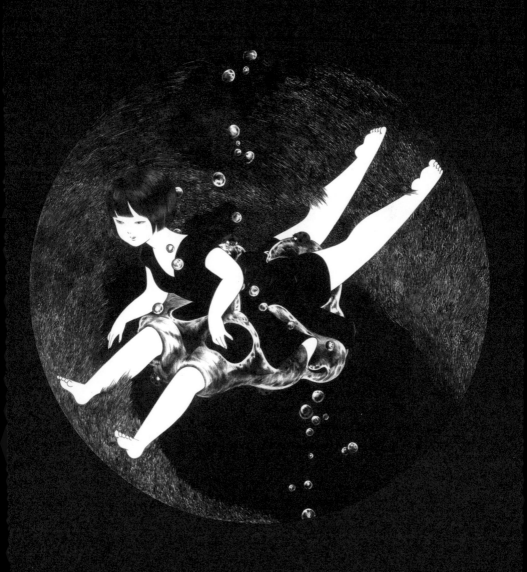

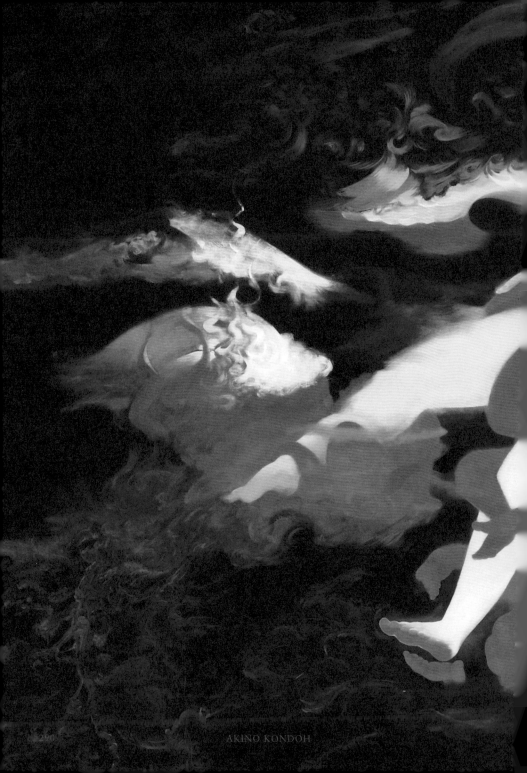

AKINO KONDOH

A.

ALICE LIN

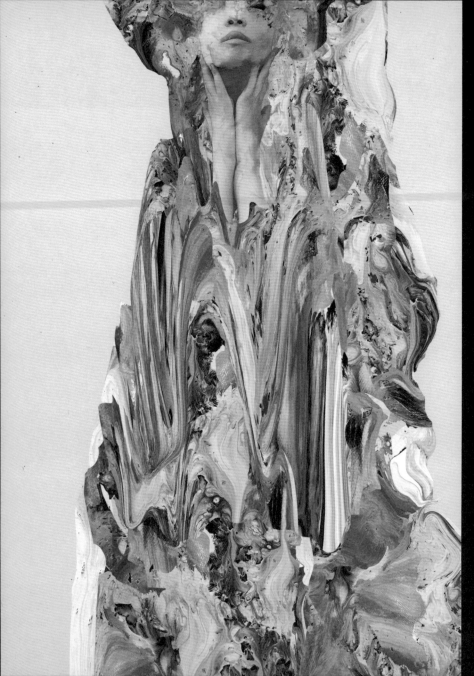

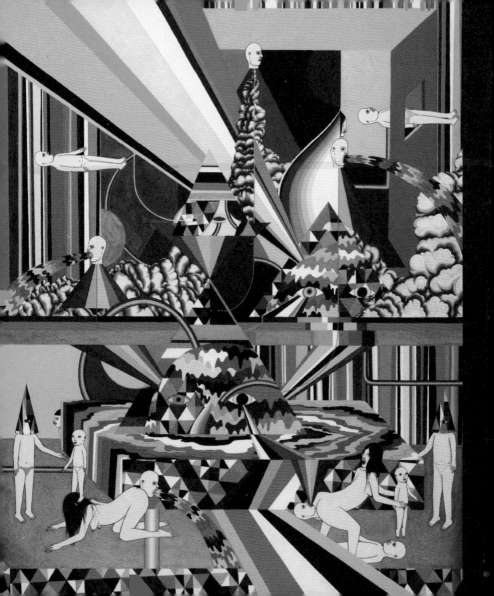

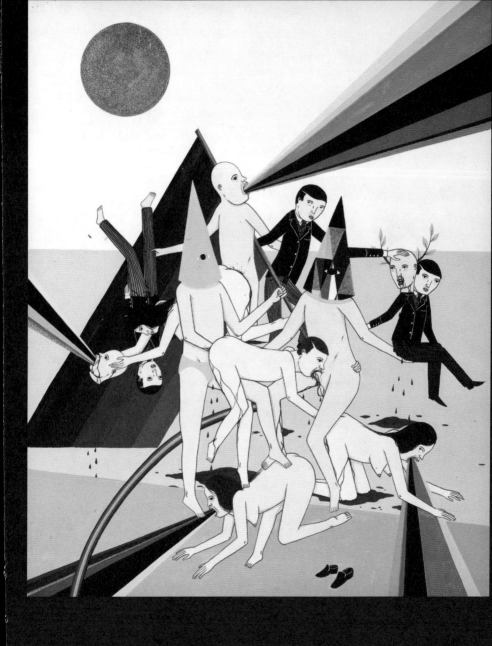

"DAMN YOU, injected vacuum formed laminate composite board with faux red cedar or light maple finish This apartment feels strange

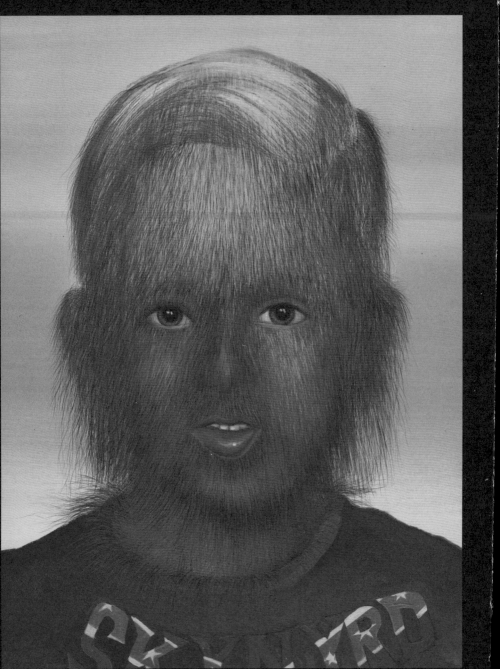

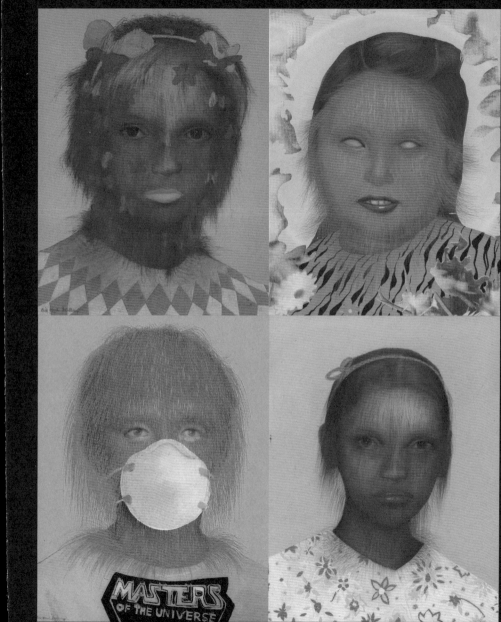

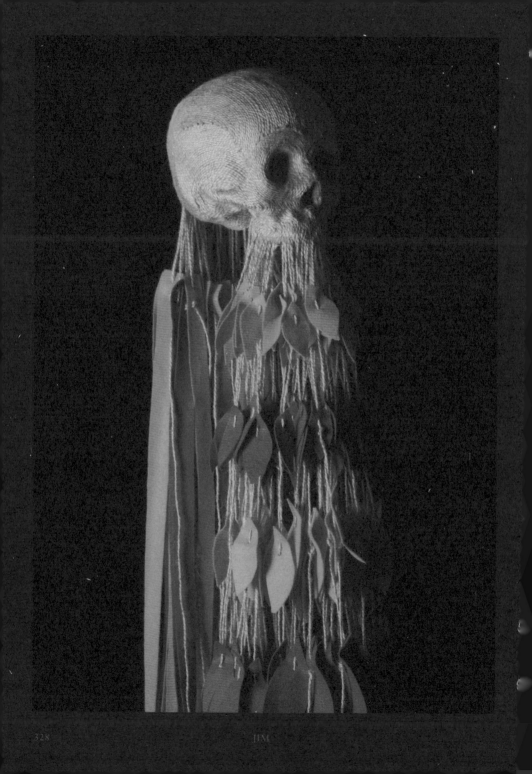

The irresponsive silence of the land,
The irresponsive sounding of the sea,
Speak both one message of one sense to me: —
Aloof, aloof, we stand aloof, so stand
Thou too aloof bound with the flawless band
Of inner solitude; we bind not thee;
But who from thy self-chain shall set thee free?
What heart shall touch thy heart? what hand thy hand?—
And I am sometimes proud and sometimes meek,
And sometimes I remember days of old
When fellowship seemed not so far to seek
And all the world and I seemed much less cold,
And at the rainbow's foot lay surely gold,
And hope felt strong and life itself not weak.

Thus am I mine own prison. Everything
Around me free and sunny and at ease:
Or if in shadow, in a shade of trees
Which the sun kisses, where the gay birds sing
And where all winds make various murmuring;
Where bees are found, with honey for the bees;
Where sounds are music, and where silences
Are music of an unlike fashioning.
Then gaze I at the merrymaking crew,
And smile a moment and a moment sigh
Thinking: Why can I not rejoice with you ?
But soon I put the foolish fancy by:
I am not what I have nor what I do;
But what I was I am, I am even I.

Therefore myself is that one only thing
I hold to use or waste, to keep or give;
My sole possession every day I live,
And still mine own despite Time's winnowing.
Ever mine own, while moons and seasons bring
From crudeness ripeness mellow and sanative;
Ever mine own, till Death shall ply his sieve;
And still mine own, when saints break grave and sing.
And this myself as king unto my King
I give, to Him Who gave Himself for me;
Who gives Himself to me, and bids me sing
A sweet new song of His redeemed set free;
He bids me sing: O death, where is thy sting?
And sing: O grave, where is thy victory?

'The Thread of Life'
by Christina Rossetti

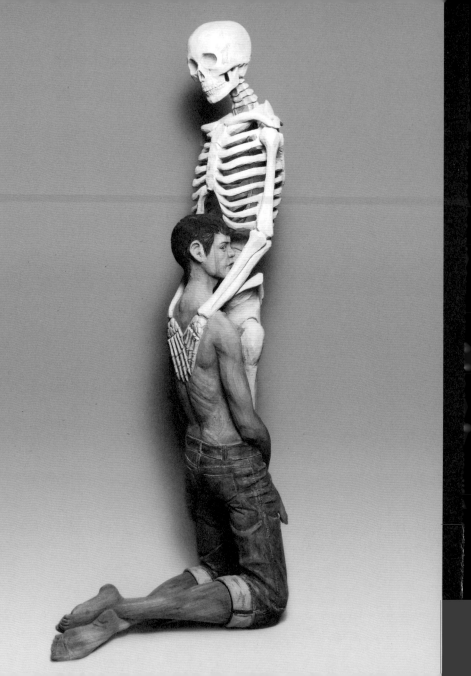

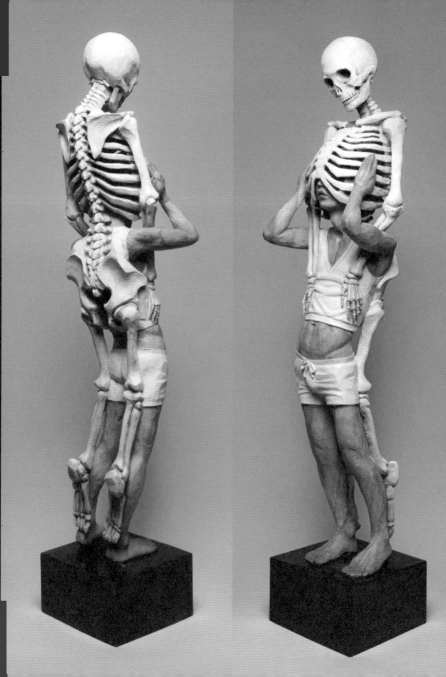

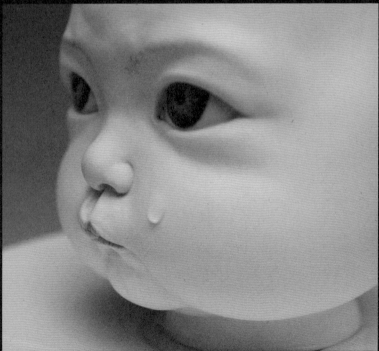

JOHNSON TSANG

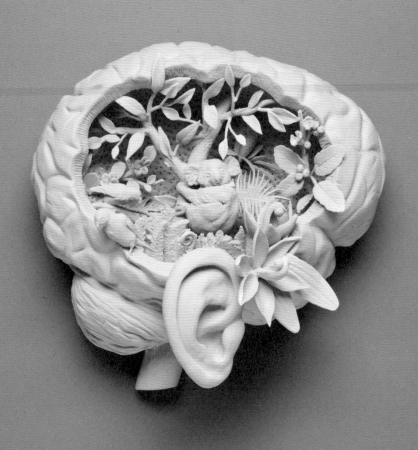

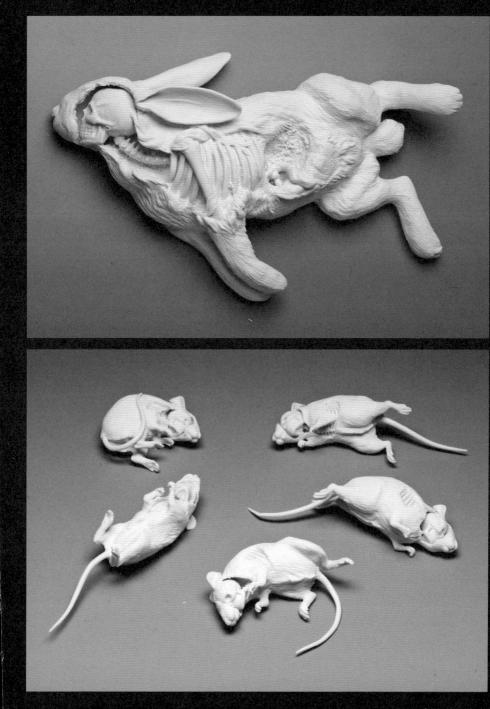

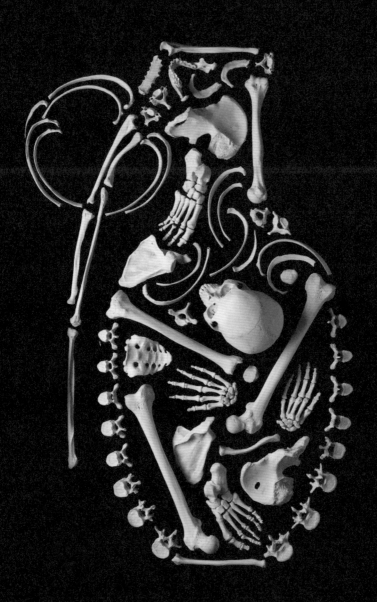

FRANCOIS ROBERT

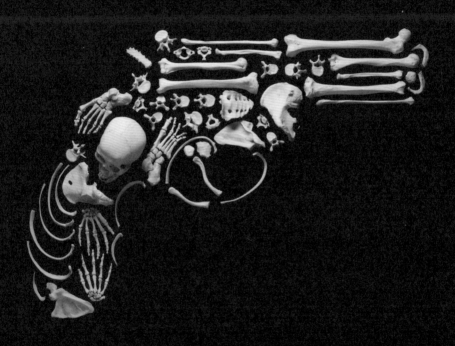

FRANCOIS ROBERT

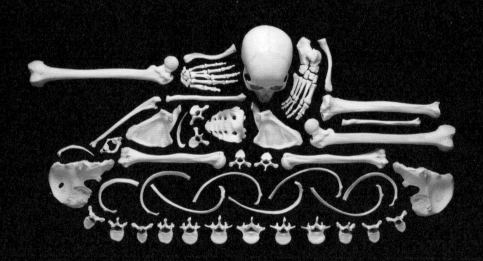

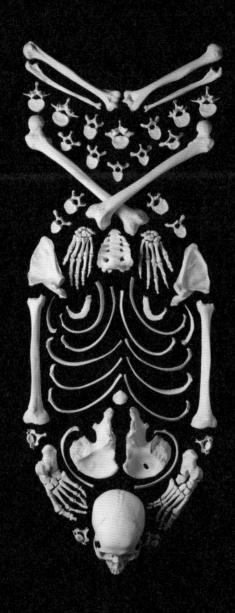

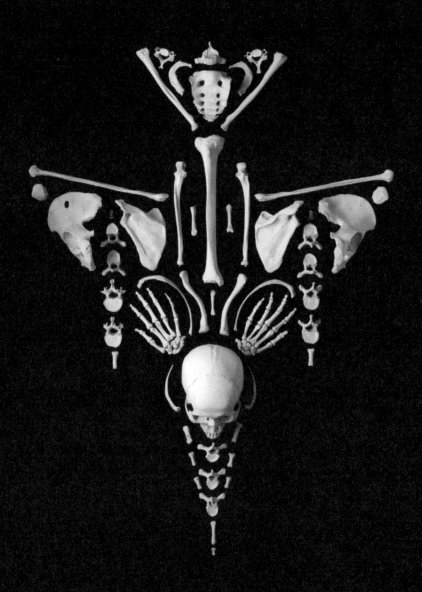

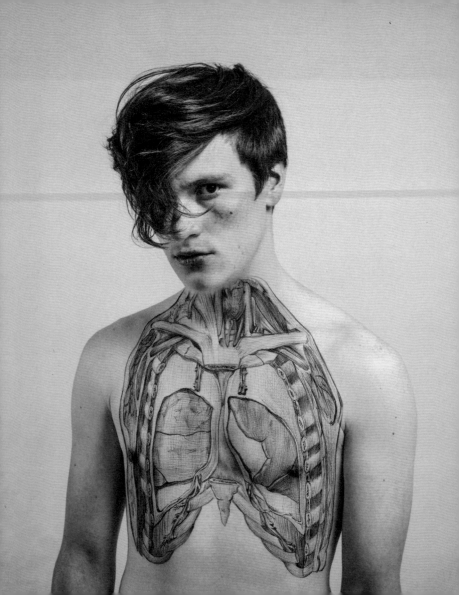

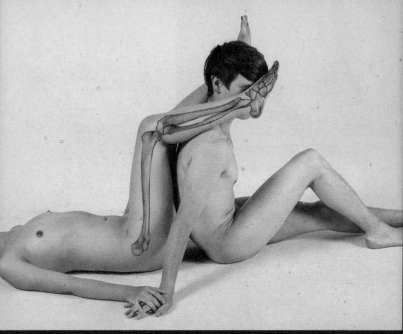

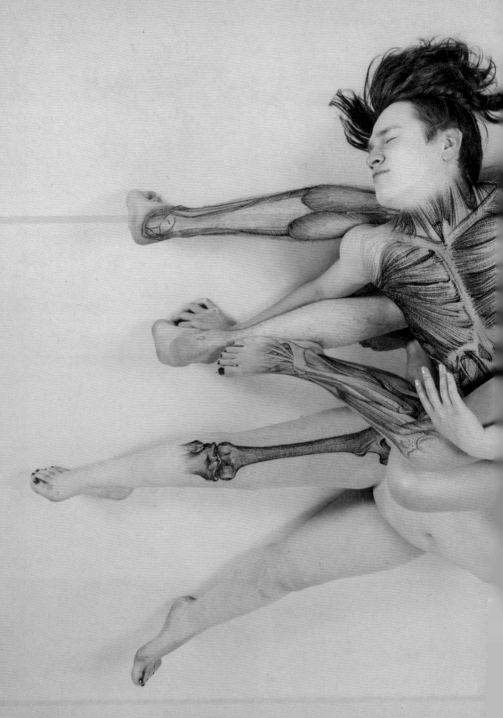

PAOLA ROJAS H & DAVID PEREZ

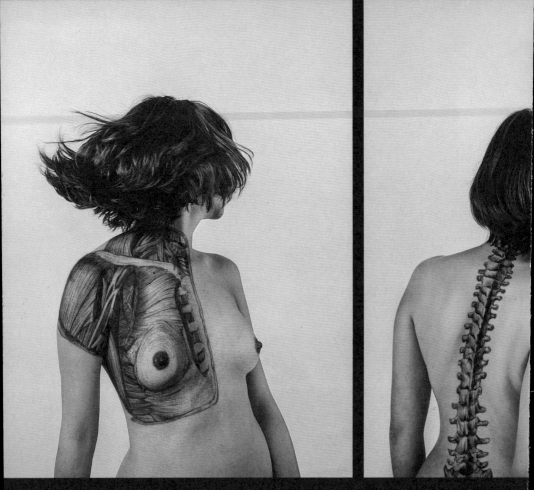

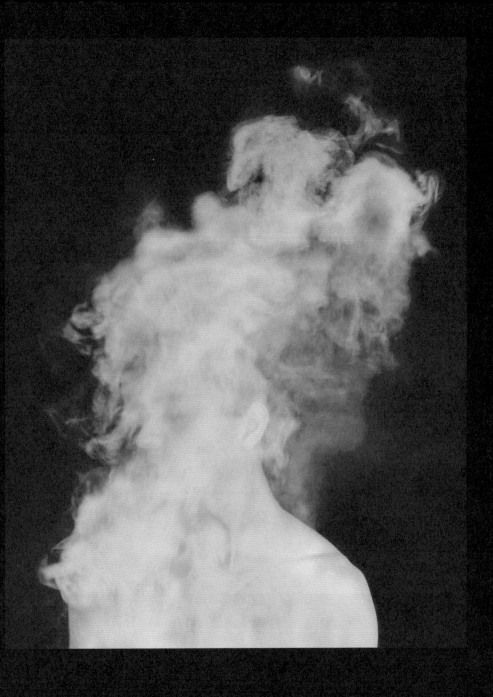

EVELYN BENCICOVA

EVELYN BENCICOVA

TILL RABUS

TILL RABUS

TILL RABUS

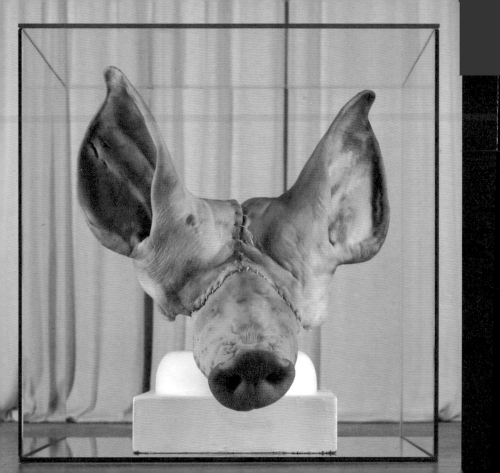

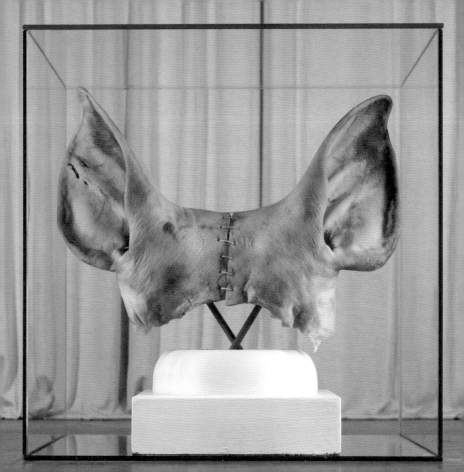

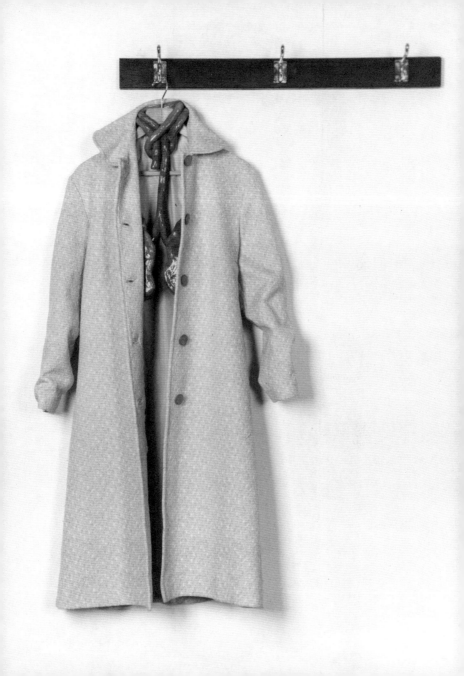

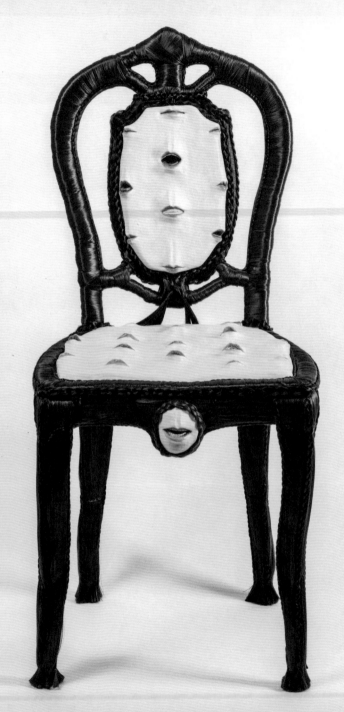

FIONA ROBERTS

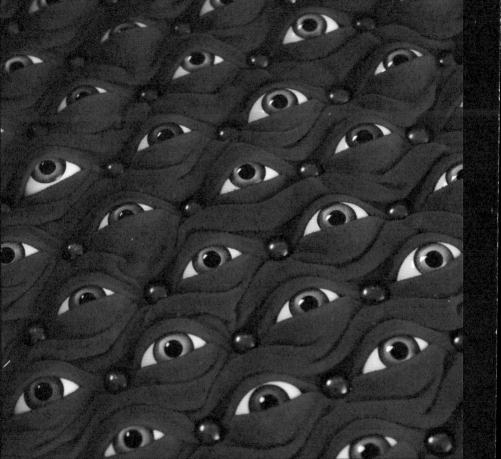

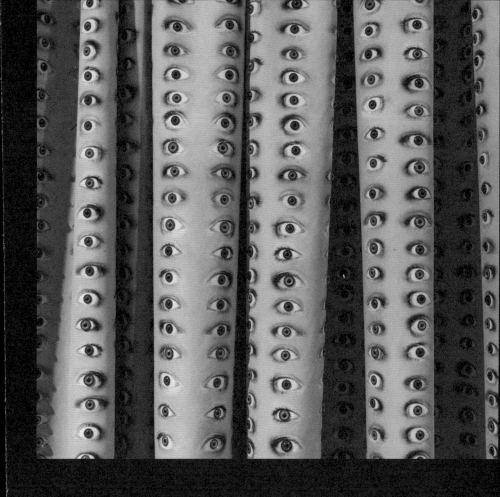

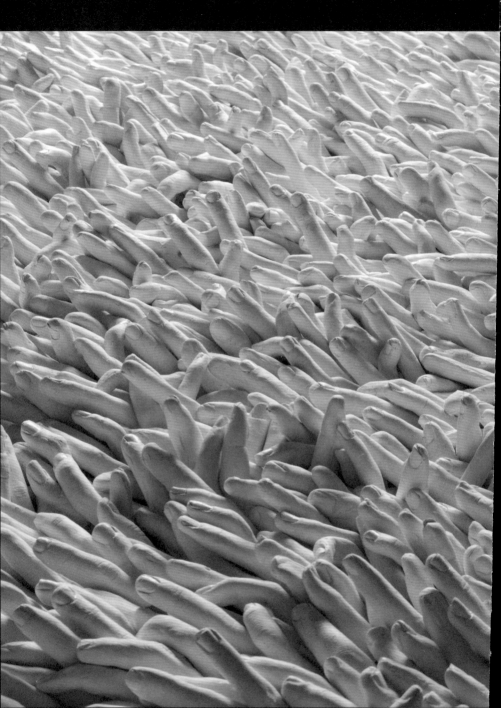

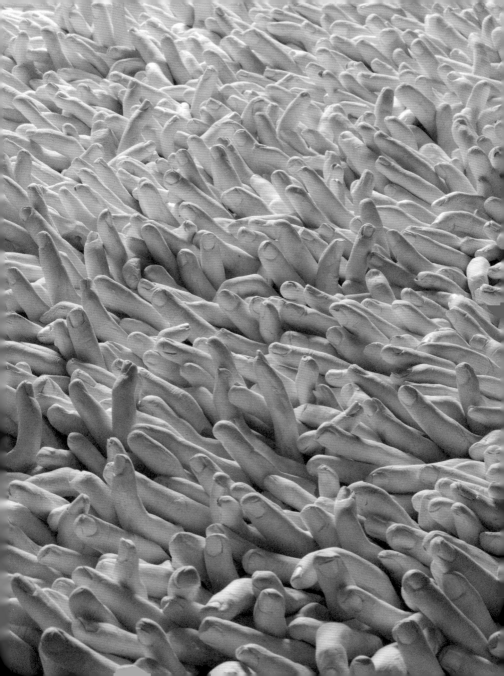

BIOGRAPHY

Aitch

Inspired by her travels, nature, childhood memories, legends and folklore, Aitch creates watercolour artwork on paper, characters cut out of wood, painted murals, intricate patterns and illustrations for clients all over the world.

Akino Kondoh

Born in Chiba in 1980, Akino Kondoh graduated from Tama Art University with a BA in Graphic Design in 2003. Her work spans various media animation, manga, drawing, painting and has been exhibited internationally.

Aleksandra Waliszewska

Aleksandra Waliszewska is a Polish painter who produces drawings and gouaches revolving around the subjects of temptation, submission and death – among others.

Alessandro Sicioldr Bianchi

Tuscania-born Alessandro Sicioldr started training in his father's studio, where he learned the methods and materials for painting and drawing. Inspired by the irrationality of surrealism and exploration of the human psyche as well as Mannerism and Flemish painters, his works represent his own interiority and subconscious.

Alex Garant

Internationally renowned as the Queen of Double Eyes, Alex Garant studied visual arts at Notre-Dame–De-Foy College. After graduating, she decided to truly commit to her passion for arts after suffering from a heart attack in 2012, changing forever how she would see the world.

Alice Lin

Born in 1980, Alice Lin is a painter, illustrator and 3D-effects artist who began studying calligraphy, Chinese painting and classical poetry as a child. Her style integrates watercolour and several Chinese techniques to express a unique wonderland of the mind and emotions.

Amandine Urruty

Urruty was born in 1982 and is currently based in Paris and Toulouse. After receiving her Master of Philosophy of Art in 2005, Urruty began exhibiting her work and working as an illustrator. Her illustrations have been exhibited in galleries throughout Europe, North America and Asia. She has published two books, Robinet d'Amour and Dommage Fromage.

Audrey Kawasaki

Shoujo manga and horror comics were the sources of influences that got Audrey Kawasaki into drawing when she was young. The Japanese-American artist spent two years studying fine art painting in Pratt Institute, before settling in Los Angeles.

Bene Rohlmann

Bene Rohlmann was born in Münster where he received a Diploma in Illustration and moved to Berlin in 2010. The artist and illustrator mostly draws inspiration from surrealism, mythology, comics, cartoons, graphics from the first half of the 20th century, and his own childhood. Filled with weirdness and dark humour, his work has been featured in local and international magazines, newspapers, and exhibitions.

P.044–049

Dadu Shin

Dadu Shin is an illustrator who attended the Rhode Island School of Design and graduated in 2010. His work has been recognised and exhibited by American Illustration, Society of Illustrators and Communication Arts.

P.185–186

Dan Hillier

Dan Hillier's career as a professional artist in Stoke Newington began when he left his job at a charity. Apart from his collages, he also produces original ink drawings with pen and ink. His work has been exhibited in various established galleries, including the Saatchi Gallery and the ICA in London; as well as solo and group shows in major cities around the world.

P.244–253

Daniel Martin Diaz

Daniel Martin Diaz is a fine artist with an insatiable curiosity to explore the mysteries of life and science. His work has been exhibited worldwide and published in the LA Times, New York Times, Juxtapoz, Hi-Fructose Magazine, Lowrider Magazine and four personal art books. He has also created artwork for large public projects and won many awards along the way.

P.258, 260–265

Danny Van Ryswyk

Danny Van Ryswyk produces paintings and 3D-printed sculptures of moody and contemplative characters, sometimes encased in glass domes, to capture the eerie feel of scientific specimens from another era. His interest in the supernatural world began after an encounter he had with a UFO when he was a young boy; leading to the creation of his mysterious world of shadows.

P.090–099

David Ho

Having experimented with media like oil, acrylics and the airbrush, California-based David Ho currently works with the help of software like Photoshop, Illustrator, Poser and Bryce. His digital artworks have been widely recognised and featured in various competitions and publications worldwide.

P.062–065

drømsjel

drømsjel or Pierre Schmidt was born in 1987 in a small city near Cologne. His work floats freely between illustration and collage, as well as traditional and digital media. The artist splices vintage photographs of well-groomed ladies and gentlemen that evoke the standards of 20th-century propriety, turning them into bastions of surreal visions.

P.142–147

Eero Lampinen

Eero Lampinen is a Helsinki-based illustrator who works with ink, brushes, watercolour and an eerie digital colour palette. His work is an intriguing blend of folklore and pop culture, often depicting offbeat characters in adjacent realities. Sugarcoated hues and modern decorative details paint the tone for his dreamlike scenarios that blur the lines between fantasy and reality.

Eika

Eika or Karina Eibatova has had a strong belief in magic, as well as a love for nature and drawing since a very young age. She is a watercolour painter, illustrator, muralist, typographer, pencil artist, and videographer who specialises in landscape art.

Elisa Ancori

Born in 1990, Elisa Ancori graduated in fine art from the University of Barcelona (2011) and illustration from Bau University (2012). Her work has been exhibited in Barcelona and Paris, in galleries such as MISCELANEA, Mutuo, Lafutura, and art fairs like GMAC and KÖLNER LISTE.

Erik Mark Sandberg

Erik Mark Sandberg obtained his BFA with distinction from Art Center College of Design in Pasadena. He has also taught at the Art Center College of Design, California State University Northridge and Otis College of Design.

Evelyn Bencicova

Born in 1992, Evelyn Bencicova is a visual creative who turned to photography after a career in modelling. She focuses on where the commercial and the artistic meet, bringing out the conceptual and visual aspects of photography to actively communicate with audiences.

Fabian Mérelle

Fabian Mérelle rediscovered his love for the shadowy world of tales upon finding his carefully preserved childhood drawings. His work references ancient myths and legends as much as major figures in art history and the traditions of anatomical drawings, interjected with the occasional pun or quote.

Fiona Roberts

Fiona Roberts' work focuses on the fragility of life and the discourse between the mind, body and home. She is a mixed media artist who uses a variety of traditional and non-traditional art materials, including ceramics, digital imaging and oil painting, as well as hair, furniture, upholstery and found objects.

Francesco Brunotti

An Italian creative who focuses on motion graphics, music videos, photography and graphic design, Francesco Brunotti has worked with agencies and international music artists, while producing personal photography projects.

Francois Robert

Known for his commercial work, La Chaux-de-Fonds-born Francois Robert's fine art photography is equally provocative, covering a wide range of subjects from evocative Polaroid transfer prints to candid street and travel shots, as well as still life.

P.346–351

Fuco Ueda

Fuco Ueda was born in 1979 and graduated from the Tokyo Polytechnic University of Arts Graduate School in 2003. Besides winning several awards locally, her work has also been exhibited internationally. Her art book, LUCID DREAM, was published in 2011.

P.308–317

Gabriel Isak

Born in Huskvarna, Gabriel Isak creates photographs that are simple in form but rich in ideas and emotions. His imagery entails surreal and melancholic scenes inspired by dreams and psychology, inviting viewers to interact with solitary figures that symbolise our own unconscious states and introspective journeys.

P.362–369

Giacomo Carmagnola

Montebelluna-born Giacomo Carmagnola studied graphic design and communication at university, but used his training to develop new illustration styles instead. He is known for his distinct take on glitch art, based on deformity and distortion.

P.100–101

Guim Tió Zarraluki

Born in Barcelona and a graduate in fine arts from the University of Barcelona, Guim Tió Zarraluki's work has been widely exhibited around the world. He is also a popular speaker at conferences and workshops..

P.152–157

Hannes Hummel

Hannes Hummel is an independent multidisciplinary designer based in Cologne. He focuses on the intersection between new technologies and traditional craft to create outstanding experiences. He has also worked on music and fashion-related projects in different mediums.

P.192–195, 330, 333

Heiko Müller

Heiko Müller's art sprouts from an urge to explore. Perhaps inspired by dark incidents behind the façade of nature or the hidden machinations within the animal kingdom, Heiko is particularly thrilled by the kind of spiritual terror expressed in old Flemish paintings, applying the mood into the serene and harmless world of rural folk art.

P.103–109

James Jean

James Jean works from Los Angeles after studying at the School of Visual Arts in New York. Publicly acclaimed for work on DC Comics cover art, he is the winner of seven Eisner Awards, three Harvey Awards and three gold medals from the Society of Illustrators. He paints on cradled wood with acrylics, oil and pastel. He held his solo exhibition 'Seven Phases' in HYBE Insight Museum in 2021.

P.034–039

Januz Miralles

Januz Miralles is a Filipino visual artist who merges photography and painting to reveal scenes from his imagination. Elusive and cryptic, his work creates fleeting but powerful emotions presented by monochromatic hues, bold strokes, and feminine shapes. Miralles is also a writer of Filippine poetry and a slave to a growing army of cats.

P.296–301

Jeff Mcmillan

1980s pop culture has had a vast influence on Jeff McMillan's work. He proclaims that the era boasted the best TV programming, cartoons, toys and movies – a decade of imagination and creativity while the world was changing drastically on all levels.

P.024–027

Jesse Auersalo

Finnish-born Jesse Auersalo is fascinated by redefining the mundane and the disposable that he surrounds himself with. He compares his work to cooking a sweet-and-sour dish, in which the dynamic gives the bitter or sweet its potency. The visual artist now dedicates most of his time to illustration.

P.204–205, 282–283

Jim

Koumac, a New Caledonian commune, was where the adventures of Jim first began. Having been marked by the diverse human, cultural and ritual experiences as he travelled around Oceania and Asia, he returned to Paris inspired in 1976. He was admitted to Estienne School and later Olivier de Serres, before creating his first skulls in 1980.

P.326–329

Johnson Tsang

Johnson Tsang is renowned for his ceramic and stainless steel sculptures. He was appointed as the Museum Expert Advisor of the Leisure and Cultural Servicess Department by the Government of Hong Kong Special Administrative Region. He also won the Special Prize at the 2011 Korea Gyeonggi International Ceramix Biennale, and the Grand Prize at the 2012 Taiwan International Ceramics Biennale.

P.338–341

Jon Beinart

Best known for his doll sculptures, Toddlerpedes, as well as detailed graphite and ink drawings, visual artist Jon Beinart also publishes art books featuring artists in the beinArt collective. Lost in his imagination since an early age and preoccupied with the lives of ants, snails, spiders and mice, he sees drawing as the fundamental element in his well-being.

P.210–213

Jules Julien

French artist Jules Julien or Julien Roure drifts and shifts in his work by questioning the reality of the world. He puts in scene a world where symbolism blends with anecdotes, and the strange is concealed behind the image – an underground world where superheroes would be called Eros and Thanatos.

P.188–191

Justin Nelson

Astoria-born Justin Nelson's work appears to be more or less a personification of the darker things in everyone, which can turn people into half-human-half-beast hybrids. He has been showing his work around in the Americas since 2008, holding his first solo show in 2009.

P.202–203

Kate Macdowell

Having spent a year and a half living and working in different countries, Kate MacDowell returned to the US in 2004 to study ceramics and flameworked glass. Inspired by her travels around Europe and Asia, her hand-built porcelain sculptures have been displayed throughout the world.

P.342–345

Katy Horan

Katy Horan was born in Houston and received a BFA from The Rhode Island School of Design in 2003. Her work has been exhibited in galleries in the Americas. She has also published several books, such as The Exquisite Book (Chronicle) and Beasts! (Fantagraphics).

P.053–054, 056–057

Kayan Kwok

The founder of a k e k e, Kayan Kwok is an artist, illustrator and graphic designer who has been living and studying between Europe, the US, and Asia. Vintage aesthetics, retro influences, pin-ups and collages inform her work. She is also fascinated by American advertisments between 1920 and 1960.

P.230–235

Kim Simonsson

Kim Simonsson graduated from the University of Art and Design Helsinki in 2000. He has been recognised as a Young Artist of the Year and invited to work for the Arabia Art Department Society, having had his work shown in private exhibitions all over the world.

P.178–183

Kotaro Chiba

Kotaro Chiba is a Japanese illustrator who started printing his illustrations on T-shirts, before illustrating commercially for books, magazines, vinyls and portraits around the world. He has also worked on branding as a graphic designer.

P.172

Lala Gallardo

Lala Gallardo has been practising art since an early age, even before she graduated from the University of the Philippines College of Fine Arts with a degree in Art History. Her art reflects her fascination for traditional indigenous crafts, as well as strange botanicals, medical biology, classic science fiction and vintage photographs.

P.050–051

Lola Dupre

Lola Dupre is a collage artist and illustrator. Working primarily with paper, her art references both the Dada aesthetic and digital manipulations. She has collaborated with brands like Nike, Jordan, and Penguin Books among many others.

P.130–135

Lostfish

Lostfish is a French artist born in 1983. Her influences are mostly classical, inspired by Flemish painters and 19th century art. She began her creative career as a self-taught freelance character designer, which later morphed into an artistic universe of digital paintings for art exhibitions. She draws mostly strange and sometimes disturbing girls who are partly woman and partly child.

P.066–069

Michael Reedy

Michael Reedy's work has been included in over 100 local and international exhibitions, as well as publications worldwide. He was born in Illinois and received a BFA in Drawing from North Central College, as well as an MFA in Painting from Northern Illinois University. He began teaching at EMU in 2005.

P.302–303

Miranda Meeks

Miranda Meeks earned a BA in Illustration at Brigham Young University in Provo. She uses both traditional and digital mediums to create dark and strange illustrations.

P.028–033

Mariana Magdaleno

The discovery of one's identity or spiritual nature, the mimesis between animals and humans, as well as the hybridisation between good and evil are recurring themes in Mariana Magdaleno's work, which has been shown in the Americas and Europe.

P.226–229

merve morkoç (Lakormis)

merve morkoç's paintings are inspired by street culture and lives. Enthused by the animations, commercials and narrative styles of urban origins that surround her, she creates alluring narrations and forms, while keeping a characteristic distance with the viewer.

P.198–201

Mia Mäkilä

Born in Norrköping in 1979, Mia Mäkilä is a self-taught artist and art historian who finds herself inspired by David Lynch, Ingmar Bergman, Terry Gilliam and Tim Burton, as well as artists like Hieronymus Bosch and Pieter Bruegel.

P.058–061

Nadja Jovanović

Born in 1983, Nadja Jovanović graduated from the University of Fine Arts in Belgrade. Her work is based on exploring aspects of existence, the presence of the individual in a moment and time, and self projections of reality. At the epicentre of her work is the person, isolated from society in a constant dualism of the conscious and unconscious.

P.120–129

Nicoletta Ceccoli

Nicoletta Ceccoli is an illustrator playing with contradictions like the dark side of a nursery rhyme or a dream of lovely things with a hint of darkness. Her whimsical yet disturbing work has been exhibited around the world.

P.110–119

Oleg Dou

With his inspiration springing from fashion culture and surrealists, Oleg Dou looks to shock people by combining reality and artificiality. The Russian photographer and digital artist has been working closely with galleries around the world since 2006.

P.206–209

Olivia Knapp

Olivia Knapp's tight cross-hatching technique involves long, slow and steady curved lines that articulate the contours of her subjects, creating a supple and tangible imagery. These unswelled lines incorporate a 'line-to-dot' rendering method, as well as an extremely rare 'dot-and-lozenge' rendering method that was used by 16th century masters. Her work explores the relationship between desire, reason, and circumstance.

P.240–243

Paola Rojas H & David Perez

Paola is a photographer from Bogotá, whose work is an exploration of elements that steals attention. She is inspired by her curiosity for daily objects, through the body, nudity, colours, space and personal experiences that lead to intimate small narratives.
David Pérez is an illustrator and graphic designer based in Bogotá. He's 22 years old and specialises in realistic portraits with ballpoint pen.

P.356–361

Paul Hollingworth

Paul Hollingworth is an Edinburgh-based conceptual photographer whose fascination with all things photographic is born out of his love for graphic design. Blurring the lines between digital photography, design and art, his work is often brought about by a natural curiosity for all things weird and wonderful.

P.254–257

Raffaello De Vito

Raffaello De Vito was born in Mirandola in 1967. He began his career as a photographer in an advertising photography agency in 1981, and lives and works in Reggio Emilia.

P.386–391

Raul Oprea aka Saddo

Romanian artist, illustrator and muralist Saddo started his artistic career by founding one of the first Romanian street art collectives, The Playground. It brought him many projects for advertising agencies, as well as collaborations with galleries worldwide. Saddo has since developed his style into more elaborate shapes, with influences from old masters from the 15th to 17th centuries, naturalistic illustrations, surrealism, religion, and mythology.

P.016–023

Richard Colman

Richard Colman graduated from the School of the Museum of Fine Arts in Boston. Since then, his work has been exhibited in galleries and art fairs in major cities in the Americas, Europe, and Asia.

P.304–307

Ryan Oliver

For his photo montages and collages, Ryan Oliver uses high fashion and lifestyle periodicals as his primary resources. His work sets out to facilitate a dialogue between the innuendo-laden visual language of fashion imagery and pornography by exchanging the implicit for the explicit.

P.148–151

Sergio Mora / Agency Rush

Sergio Mora's work is an audacious kaleidoscope: punchy, mind-altering and colourful. Born in Barcelona, where he has lived, painted, experimented, played and created, he is a multidisciplinary artist whose prolific work takes audiences to subversive worlds, featuring beautiful monsters and grotesque fantasies in a variety of aspects.

P.272–275

Tara McPherson

Creating art about people and their oddities, Tara McPherson's characters seem to exude an idealised innocence with a glimpse of hard-earned wisdom. Recalling issues from childhood and good old life experience, she creates images that are thought-provoking and seductive. Themes of people and their interrelationships are prominent throughout her work.

P.040–043

Till Rabus

Till Rabus was born in Neuchâtel and graduated from the Ecole des Beaux-Arts in La Chaux-de-Fonds. He now lives and works in Neuchâtel. All his images are courtesy of Gallery Aeroplastics.

P.378–385

Tim Lee

Tim Lee was born into an artistic family, with a great-grandfather notable for his childlike illustrations and uncles well-respected in their fields of pottery and fine art. His interest in art sprouted at an early age, leading to the creation of his Chinese ink drawing series on traditional rice paper in 2008. His work is a fascinating dichotomy of cultures, combining his love for Chinese history and knowledge of Western art.

P.284–285

Yido

Yido, for Yes I do Concept, is the pseudonym of Enrique Núñez. Born in Benicàssim in 1977, his work covers a wide range of fields, through which he tries to convey different meanings.

P.236–239

Yoshitoshi Kanemaki

Yoshitoshi Kanemaki grew up in the Chiba prefecture and graduated from the Department of Sculpture at Tama Art University in Tokyo. He has loved origami, constellations and GUNDAM models since childhood, using camphor to express the feelings of being human in his work.

P.334–337

Yuka Yamaguchi

Yuka Yamaguchi was born in Kobe and has always found drawing to be a fun thing to do. The self-taught artist began drawing 'more seriously' in 2006, by intuitively and honestly transforming the exact images in her mind with colour pencils. She started exhibiting her work in 2004.

P.162–165

Yury Ustsinau

Yury Ustsinau is a Frankfurt-based designer, artist and illustrator from Vitebsk whose art began with traditional illustrations, which have since evolved. He combines faces and hands to create his surrealistic world rendered in black and white. Yury holds a degree in product design from Vitebsk State Technological University.

P.276–281

Zhou Fan

Born in 1983, Zhou Fan has always been obsessed with the idea that reality and dreams intertwine in real life. To him, dreams are not just hallucinations, but even more tangible than physical things. Subconsciously, he has always been chasing his dreams through his paintings, revealing their interconnectedness with reality.

P.166–171